诸子百家国风画传
The Pictorial Biographies of Great Thinkers

图/忻秉勇
文/肖霞
译/秦悦

孙子画传

SUNZI

济南出版社

图书在版编目（CIP）数据

孙子画传 / 忻秉勇著. —— 济南：济南出版社, 2015.12
(诸子百家国风画传)
ISBN 978-7-5488-2001-7

Ⅰ. ①孙… Ⅱ. ①忻… Ⅲ. ①孙武－传记－画册Ⅳ.
① K825.2-64

中国版本图书馆CIP数据核字(2016)第011643号

◆图/忻秉勇　◆文/肖　霞　◆译/秦　悦

◎"原动力"中国原创动漫出版扶持计划入选项目
◎上海市重大文艺创作项目由上海文化发展基金会资助
◎上海市文化"走出去"项目由上海市文化"走出去"专项扶持资金赞助

## 孙子画传

| 出版发行 | 济南出版社 |
|---|---|
| 总 执 行 | 上海海派连环画中心 |
| | 上海城市动漫出版传媒有限公司 |
| | 济南出版有限责任公司 |
| 图书策划 | 刘　军　刘亚军 |
| 出版策划 | 崔　刚　朱孔宝 |
| 出版执行 | 张承军 |
| 责任编辑 | 张雪丽 |
| 特约编辑 | 张永祥　刘蓉蓉　余　阳　路艳艳 |
| 装帧设计 | 舒晓春　焦萍萍 |

| 印　　刷 | 济南鲁艺彩印有限公司 |
|---|---|
| 开　　本 | 210×285　1/16 |
| 印　　张 | 5.75 |
| 字　　数 | 90千字 |
| 版　　次 | 2015年12月第1版 |
| 印　　次 | 2016年2月第1次印刷 |
| 标准书号 | ISBN 978-7-5488-2001-7 |
| 定　　价 | 45.00元 |

济南版图书，如有印装错误，可随时调换。

# 诸子百家国风画传
## 编委会

| | |
|---|---|
| 总　顾　问 | 徐麟 |
| 编委会主任 | 朱咏雷 |
| 编委会副主任 | 陈静溪　高韵斐　王世农　何彧　徐慧玲 |
| 编委会委员 | 汤世芬　丁绍敏　赵钢　梅花　张夏 |
| | 张鸿　夏凡　殷涛　王廷文　钱斐 |
| | 刘军　崔刚　邵炳军　刘亚军　占剑 |
| | 朱孔宝　曹奕 |
| 学术顾问 | 傅璇琮 |
| 总　策　划 | 上海市人民政府新闻办公室 |
| 联　合　策划 | 上海报业集团 |
| | 山东省人民政府新闻办公室 |
| | 河南省人民政府新闻办公室 |
| | 中国儒学馆（浙江衢州） |
| 总　执　行 | 上海城市动漫出版传媒有限公司 |
| | 上海海派连环画中心 |
| | 济南出版有限责任公司 |
| 联　合　执行 | 曲阜市人民政府新闻办公室 |
| | 邹城市人民政府新闻办公室 |
| | 商丘市人民政府新闻办公室 |
| | 鹿邑县人民政府新闻办公室 |
| | 滕州市人民政府新闻办公室 |
| | 广饶孙子文化研究中心 |

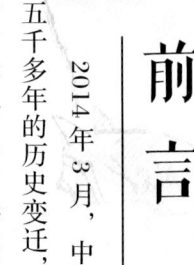

# 前言

2014年3月，中国国家主席习近平在联合国教科文组织总部的演讲中指出：「中华文明经历了五千多年的历史变迁，但始终一脉相承，积淀着中华民族最深层的精神追求，代表着中华民族独特的精神标识，为中华民族生生不息、发展壮大提供了丰厚滋养。」中华传统文化是潺潺流水，润物无声，滋养了世代中国人的精神家园。在中华传统文化波澜壮阔的历史画卷中，诸子百家文化就是其中浓墨重彩的一页。

充满先贤智慧的诸子百家文化，是集中华传统文化、哲学、艺术于一体的文明宝藏：反对暴力，期盼人与人之间和睦相处、以礼相待，这是儒家思想的「仁」；平等博爱，止息不义战争，这是墨家思想的「兼爱非攻」；遵循自然、万物和谐，这是道家思想的「道法自然」；论兵却主张「不战而屈人之兵」，这是充满智慧光芒的兵家思想……诸子百家的思想，正包含着人们所努力构造的幸福世界中的重要基石。这是中华民族的财富，也是世界文明的重要组成部分。

近代以来，上海作为中华文明走向世界的一个重要窗口，担当着向世界展示中国文化华彩精粹的重要使命。建设充满活力的国际文化大都市，上海更需要放眼全球、放眼全国，以「海纳百川」的精神打造中华文化精品，推动中华文化走向世界。

这套由国务院新闻办公室支持，上海市政府新闻办公室、河南省政府新闻办公室协力出版的《诸子百家国风画传》丛书，化繁难为轻逸、化艰深为平易，充满了思想美、故事美、人性美、艺术美。它将诸子思想中的妙笔华章与国画家的水墨丹青巧妙结合，书香墨趣将诸子的音容笑貌、神采风骨生动地呈现在读者面前。它向世界打开了中华传统文化之门，同时也为中华文化拓展国际文化交流，进行了新的尝试和创新，提供了新的载体和通道。

诸子百家文化精神正如追逐理性、自由与美的古希腊人文精神一般，是人类共同的文化财富。希望诸位读者从这套书出发，分享故事，体验艺术，感悟哲理，开始一段美不胜收的中华传统文化探源之旅。灿如云霞的中华文化让世人心向往之。

二〇一四年九月

# Preface

In March of 2014, President Xi Jinping pointed out in his speech delivered in the headquarters of UNESCO, "Having gone through over 5000 years of vicissitudes, the Chinese civilization has always kept to its original root. Unique in representing China spiritually, it contains some most profound pursuits of the Chinese nation and provides it with abundant nourishment for existence and development." The Chinese traditional culture is just like trickling water irrigating and nurturing the spiritual realm of Chinese people. In the long and splendid picture of Chinese cultural history, the contributions of great thinkers are the most glorious chapter.

The wisdom and philosophies of these great thinkers crystallized culture, philosophy and art in our Chinese civilization: Confucian "benevolence", Mohist "universal love", Taoist "modeling itself after Nature" and the military teaching about "attaining victory in war without fighting" are still holding the stage. These fascinating thoughts constitute the cornerstones of an ideal world that Chinese people dream of having. These spiritual assets not only belong to Chinese people but also constitute an integral part of the world civilization.

As an important window in modern times, Shanghai has assumed a mission to demonstrate the brilliance of Chinese culture. To construct a dynamic international cultural metropolis and to promote Chinese culture to the world, Shanghai needs a mind so open to the entire country and entire world and a mind so tolerant as the vast ocean admitting hundreds of rivers.

*The Pictorial Biographies of Great Thinkers* supported by The State Council Information Office and Information Office of Shanghai Municipality is a close cooperation between Information Office of Shandong Provincial People's Government and Information Office of Henan Provincial People's Government. This series in Chinese painting style simplified the complicated history into simple stories, revealing the beauty of human nature as well as artistic creation. The ink painting presented vividly the personalities of great thinkers, attracting readers to explore their great thoughts and ideas. The pictorial biographies helped open the door of Chinese traditional culture to the world, and this attempt also provided a new carrier and channel for cultural exchange.

The brilliant Chinese culture is fascinating. Like the pursuit for reason, freedom and beauty in ancient Greek humanism, the legacy from these great thinkers is also the cultural assets shared by the whole humanity. It is hoped that readers can embark on a journey to explore traditional Chinese culture through reading these books.

September 2014

# 编者的话

《史记》有云：世俗所称师旅，皆道《孙子》十三篇。《孙子兵法》被誉为中国古代军事"圣典"，也是孙子（即孙武）的遗世之作。孙子的军事思想蕴含着对待战争的智慧，提倡"不战而屈人之兵"的王者之道，用"齐文化"的理念将竞争规为有序。孙子的哲学思想长盛不衰，直至今日仍活跃于军事、政治、商业等领域，更深深地融入中华民族爱好和平、不畏强权的民族性格中。

《孙子画传》旨在描述孙子生平故事：年少隐居耕读的淡泊明志，吴国斩姬练兵的正直刚毅，行军作战的智计频传……从这些场景中，呈现出孙子的人格魅力与处世智慧。国画家忻秉勇妙手丹青，笔墨交错构成的配图典雅耐读，既与文字相得益彰，又通过生动的细节、场景拓展了叙事空间。

《孙子画传》缩影了真实的孙子，展现了春秋时代恢宏的战争场景，表达了战与和协调平衡的兵家思想，是了解孙子、了解中华民族传统文化的良册。

## Editor's Note

*In Records of the Historian*, Sima Qian claimed, when people payed a compliment about the military tactics, they all complimented the 13 articles of *The Art of War*. *The Art of War* is a treasure Sunzi (named Sun Wu) left to us and it has always been esteemed as a classical military work though written in the ancient China. Sunzi's military thoughts advocate "subduing the enemy without involving actual fighting" and its regulating military competition with Qi culture contains a great deal of wisdom about war. Sunzi's philosophy has been applied in the military, political and commercial fields, and has long been embedded in our peace-loving and power-defying Chinese character.

*Sunzi* is a pictorial account of Sunzi's life: reading and farming in seclusion, beheading the king's favorite concubines, training rigorously, and commanding the army… All these episodes show Sunzi's charisma and wisdom. Mr. Xin Bingyong's painting, with its deft brush and ink, and the fraction of space and shape, best illustrates and completes the captions. His handling of details and settings help to expand the narrative possibility.

*Sunzi* not only presents a real Sunzi and the grand scale wars during the Spring and Autumn Period, it also conveys a military concept of maintaining a balance between war and peace. *Sunzi* is a must-read through which one can get to know Sunzi and the traditional Chinese culture.

# 目录 Contents

| | |
|---|---|
| 兵圣名垂青史图 | An eternal glory — 02 |
| 孙武先祖占卜图 | Ancestors practising divination — 04 |
| 田完齐国发迹图 | Tian Wan rising to fame in the State of Qi — 06 |
| 世胄启蒙悟兵图 | Showing interest in the art of war — 08 |
| 孙武隐居耕读图 | Sun Wu reading and farming in seclusion — 10 |
| 武、胥姑苏结交图 | Sun Wu making friends with Wu Zixu in Gusu city — 12 |
| 姬光谋刺王僚图 | Duke Liao's assassination — 14 |
| 吴王阖闾登基图 | Duke Helyu ascending the throne — 16 |
| 子胥举荐孙武图 | Wu Zixu recommending Sun Wu — 18 |
| 兵圣孙武图（一） | Sun Wu: The Ultimate Master of War (1) — 20 |
| 孙子拜会吴王图 | Sunzi's audience with Duke Helyu — 22 |
| 阖闾姬试孙武图 | Duke Helyu demanding a drill — 24 |
| 兵场喧哗围观图 | The excited spectators of the drill — 26 |
| 宫中佳丽列队图 | Maids in the drill — 28 |
| 演前孙子立规图 | Sunzi explaining the rules for drill — 30 |
| 宫女嬉笑乱阵图 | Playful carelessness in the drill — 32 |
| 孙子训斥宠姬图 | Sunzi criticizing the concubines — 34 |
| 孙子击鼓指挥图 | Sunzi beating the drum to command — 36 |
| 孙子拒情斩姬图 | The captains beheaded — 38 |
| 宫女整齐练兵图 | A real drill — 40 |
| 孙子辞别吴王图 | Sunzi bidding farewell to Duke Helyu — 42 |
| 吴王纳谏释嫌图 | Duke Helyu and Sun Wu settling differences — 44 |
| 孙子练兵强国图 | Sun Wu training the troops — 46 |
| 吴国兴兵伐楚图 | The State of Wu attacking the State of Chu — 48 |
| 孙子疲楚变易图 | Sunzi waiting for the timing — 50 |
| 子常索贿蒙君图 | Zichang asking for bribes — 52 |
| 蔡、唐贡宝救主图 | Tributes paid for a journey home — 54 |
| 孙子献策奇袭图 | Sunzi' s proposal — 56 |
| 吴楚夹岸对峙图 | The troops of Wu confronting the troops of Chu — 58 |
| 兵圣孙武图（二） | Sun Wu: The Ultimate Master of War (2) — 60 |
| 诱敌深入决战图 | Luring the enemy in deep — 62 |
| 孙、伍备战柏举图 | Sunzi and Wu Zixu planning for the coming battle in Boju — 64 |
| 夫概孤勇出战图 | Fugai leading the fight — 66 |
| 乘胜追击溃楚图 | Defeating Chu with victorious pursuit — 68 |
| 包胥秦庭哭救图 | Baoxu crying for help — 70 |
| 吴王回师平叛图 | A coup at home — 72 |
| 孙子功名受托图 | Entrusting the care of Fuchai — 74 |
| 孙、伍辅吴称霸图 | Wu being the dominant power with the two assistants — 76 |
| 兵圣兵书流芳图 | The Art of War — 78 |
| 王者之道普世图 | Words of wisdom — 80 |

◎兵圣名垂青史图
An eternal glory

兵者，国之大事，死生之地，存亡之道，不可不察也。
（《孙子兵法·计篇》）

孙武，字长卿，后人尊称其为孙子，生卒年不详，约与孔子同时而稍晚。他是舜帝苗裔，陈国公子陈完七世孙。孙武凭借一部《孙子兵法》和一次以少胜多的著名战役——吴楚柏举之战而名垂青史，史称"兵圣"。

Sun Wu, style name Changqing, respectably called Sunzi. Though his birth and death are unknown, he is believed to be a contemporary of Confucius' but years younger. He was a descendant of Emperor Shun's Miao branch, and the seventh generation of Prince Chen Wan of Chen State. Sun Wu won an eternal glory in history with *The Art of War* and a battle between the State of Wu and the State of Chu in a place called Boju, where he defeated Chu much outnumbering his troop. He is known as "The Ultimate Master of War" in history.

◎孙武先祖占卜图
Ancestors practising divination

善守者，藏于九地之下；善攻者，动于九天之上。故能自保而全胜也。
（《孙子兵法·形篇》）

陈国是上古舜帝的后裔，姓妫。春秋初期，陈厉公太子完出生时，周太史恰巧经过陈国。周王室的太史都擅长占卜之术，因此陈厉公请他占卜儿子的未来。占卜的卦象非常奇特，是"观"卦的变卦"否"卦。内容大意是：这个孩子前程远大，妫氏之后的发扬光大就全靠他了；但这不会发生在他身上，而是应验在他后代身上；不会发生在陈国，而是在姜姓之国。

The people in the State of Chen surnamed Gui, were all descendants of Emperor Shun. At the beginning of the Spring and Autumn Period when Chen Wan, the prince of Duke Li of Chen was born, an official of Zhou Dynasty who was in charge of recording history visited Chen. The official was good at the art of divination. Duke Li thus requested the official to see the divination for his son. The result of the divination was very unusual: this is a child with great expectation and may become a minister; the Gui family's aspirations can be up to him. But he himself will not fulfill these promises but his offspring would, and not in the State of Chen, but in a state governed by Jiang clan.

◎田完齐国发迹图
Tian Wan rising to fame in the State of Qi

激水之疾，至于漂石者，势也；鸷鸟之疾，至于毁折者，节也。是故善战者，其势险，其节短。（《孙子兵法·势篇》）

陈国宫廷内乱，陈厉公被杀，陈完逃亡到齐国。齐桓公知道陈完出身高贵，而且很有才能，想重用他为齐国之卿。陈完坚决推辞，于是齐桓公就任用他为工正（管理工匠的官）。由于他受赐的采邑在田，所以又称为田完。齐国大夫懿仲觉得田完是个人才，想把自己的女儿嫁给他。他请人占卜吉凶，结果十分吉利，说田完的后代在齐国一定会非常兴旺发达。懿仲就把女儿嫁给了田完。

Duke Li was killed in a civil strife in the court and Chen Wan fled to the State of Qi. Considering Chen Wan was of noble origin, Duke Huan of Qi wanted to make him a high-ranking official, but Chen Wan declined. Duke Huan then nominated him as an administrator of craftsmen. As his granted fiefdom was in the place of Tian, Chen Wan was also known as Tian Wan.

Yizhong, a senior official in Qi, thought highly of Tian Wan and wanted to marry his daughter to him. He tried to find out Tian Wan's lot by divination, and the result turned out to be very favorable: Tian Wan's offspring will thrive in Qi. Hence Yizhong married his daughter to Tian Wan.

◎世胄启蒙悟兵图
Showing interest in the art of war

兵者，诡道也。故能而示之不能，用而示之不用，近而示之远，远而示之近。利而诱之，乱而取之，实而备之，强而避之，怒而挠之，卑而骄之，佚而劳之，亲而离之。攻其无备，出其不意。（《孙子兵法·计篇》）

田氏在齐国发展到第六代，已经站稳了脚跟。孙武的祖父田书兄弟二人，在齐国位居大夫，势力很大。公元前523年，田书在攻打莒国的战役中立下大功，齐景公赐姓孙，因此田书又叫孙书。另外，齐景公还把乐安赐给他做采邑。孙武的父亲孙凭，官做得更大。生长在这样的家庭环境中，孙武不但受到了很好的教育，而且在长辈的影响下对兵法产生了浓厚的兴趣。

The Tians acquired a firm foothold in Qi in their sixth generation. Sun Wu's grandfather Tian Shu and his brother were powerful senior officials in Qi. In 523 B. C., Tian Shu won a battle against the State of Ju, and Duke Jing of Qi granted him a surname Sun, so Tian Shu was also known as Sun Shu. In addition, Duke Jing made Le'an as his fiefdom. Sun Wu's father, Sun Ping, made up to a higher position. Sun Wu received a very good education in such a family, and showed a very strong interest in the art of war.

◎孙武隐居耕读图
Sun Wu reading and farming in seclusion

故用兵之法,高陵勿向,背丘勿逆,佯北勿从,锐卒勿攻,饵兵勿食,归师勿遏,围师遗阙,穷寇勿迫,此用兵之法也。(《孙子兵法·军争篇》)

齐国田氏、鲍氏、栾氏、高氏四大家族为争夺权势发生内斗,孙武不愿纠缠其间,就避难来到了吴国。按照惯例,逃亡到其他诸侯国的贵族子弟还可以继续做官。但孙武到吴国并未投靠吴王,而是在吴国都城姑苏的城外山中隐居下来。孙武一边耕读自乐,一边潜心研究历代战争的经验教训,著述兵书。

The Tians, the Baos, the Luans, and the Gaos fought against each other for more power, but Sun Wu did not want to get involved in. He went to the State of Wu to seek peace. By convention then, the nobles in exile could also be officials in the host state. But Sun Wu did not go to the duke of Wu to ask for any post. Instead, he lived in seclusion in the suburb of Gusu city, Wu's capital. Enjoying farming and reading, he immersed himself in studying the wars of past ages and writing military articles.

◎武、胥姑苏结交图
Sun Wu making friends with Wu Zixu in Gusu city

奇正相生，如环之无端，孰能穷之哉？（《孙子兵法·势篇》）

陶醉于青山绿水与兵法世界中的孙武，就在这风光如画的姑苏城，结识了历史上同样大名鼎鼎的伍子胥。伍子胥，名员，贵族出身。其父伍奢，德高望重，是楚平王太子建的太傅（第一导师）。太子建还有一位少傅（第二导师）叫费无忌。由于平时不受太子重视，费无忌对伍奢非常嫉妒，便想方设法陷害太子、除掉伍奢。楚平王听信谗言，赶走太子，并杀害了伍子胥的父亲伍奢。伍子胥的哥哥伍尚在这次事件中也未能幸免于难。伍子胥历尽艰辛逃到吴国，投到了吴王僚的堂兄——公子姬光的门下，同时暗中结识英雄豪杰，以备将来之用。

Sun Wu got to know Wu Zixu in the picturesque Gusu city while indulging in the military world. Wu Zixu, named Yun, was born in a noble family. His father, Wu She, was a well-esteemed scholar and was a mentor of the crown prince of the State of Chu. The crown prince had another mentor Fei Wuji. Fei Wuji was not in favor and was very jealous of Wu She, so he found ways to frame the crown prince and tried to get rid of Wu She. Having believed what Fei Wuji said, Duke Ping of Chu banished the crown prince and killed Wu She. Wu Zixu's elder brother Wu Shang was also killed. Wu Zixu went through all the hardship and made his way to the State of Wu. He threw himself into the lap of the duke of Wu's cousin Ji Guang, and at the same time he associated with heroes for his future revenge.

◎ 姬光谋刺王僚图
**Duke Liao's assassination**

攻而必取者，攻其所不守也；守而必固者，守其所不攻也。故善攻者，敌不知其所守；善守者，敌不知其所攻。（《孙子兵法·虚实篇》）

周敬王五年（前515），在伍子胥的策划下，姬光在家设宴招待吴王僚。宴会上，伍子胥的结拜兄弟专诸将一把名叫"鱼肠"的匕首藏在鱼肚内，端到吴王僚面前，突然拔出匕首刺杀了吴王僚。

In the fifth year under the reign of King Jing of Zhou Dynasty (515 B. C.), Ji Guang entertained Duke Liao in his place according to Wu Zixu's plan. At the banquet, Wu Zixu's sworn brother Zhuan Zhu killed the duke with a dagger hidden in a fish dish presented to the duke.

◎吴王阖闾登基图
Duke Helyu ascending the throne

故善战人之势,如转圆石于千仞之山者,势也。(《孙子兵法·势篇》)

姬光除掉了政治对手吴王僚后,登上王位。这就是后来鼎鼎大名的吴王阖闾。吴王阖闾是一位雄才大略的君主,一心想富强吴国,称霸天下。他想重用伍子胥和另一个从楚国逃难来的贵族公子伯嚭,但又担心二人一心复仇,不顾吴国长远利益。

Getting rid of his political rival Duke Liao, Ji Guang ascended the throne. Ji Guang was the later Duke Helyu of Wu. Duke Helyu was very ambitious, and he wanted to build a strongest country. He wanted to put Wu Zixu and another noble Bo Pi who escaped from Chu in a more important position, but he was concerned at the same time that they were so determined to take revenge that they might do so at the cost of Wu's long-term goal.

◎子胥举荐孙武图
Wu Zixu recommending Sun Wu

故善战者，立于不败之地，而不失敌之败也。（《孙子兵法·形篇》）

吴王举棋不定，登台长啸，群臣没人知道阖闾的心思。伍子胥深晓吴王之意，借与吴王论兵的机会，向吴王推荐孙武。吴王陷入沉思，将军是非常重要的职位，平凡之辈难以胜任。吴王阖闾很难相信一个名不见经传的隐士能够成为叱咤疆场的将军。伍子胥深信自己的眼光，他一天之内七次向吴王推荐孙武，说："有没有才能，一试便知。"吴王拗不过子胥，答应一见。

Duke Helyu of Wu was indecisive and no one knew why. Wu Zixu understood what was going on in the duke's mind, and recommended Sun Wu when he and the duke were discussing the art of war. The duke lost in deep thoughts: a general is a very demanding position, and no ordinary man can live up to it. Duke Helyu found it hard to believe that someone obscure would be able to win overwhelming victory in the battlefield. Wu Zixu was very confident in his discernment. He recommended Sun Wu to Duke Helyu seven times within a day, saying, "Give him a chance." The duke could not refuse any more and granted an audience with Sun Wu.

◎孙子拜会吴王图
Sunzi's audience with Duke Helyu

夫将者，国之辅也，辅周则国必强，辅隙则国必弱。（《孙子兵法·谋攻篇》）

孙武觐见吴王阖闾。吴王询问了孙武的家庭背景，感到很满意。他又问及行军打仗之法，孙武早有准备，献上自己写的十三篇兵法作品。吴王一见，大为折服，每读一篇，都赞不绝口。他一边读，一边喃喃自语："此人有如此高深的兵学思想，不知实际用兵能力如何？"

Duke Helyu asked about Sun Wu's family background and seemed to be satisfied. Then the duke tested him on the art of war. Sun Wu presented the 13 articles he wrote on military strategies. Duke Helyu was deeply impressed and was in awe of his talent. The duke murmured while reading, "This man has a profound knowledge about war. But I'm not sure how well he can command a troop."

◎阖闾姬试孙武图
Duke Helyu demanding a drill

善用兵者，修道而保法，故能为胜败之政。（《孙子兵法·形篇》）

吴王想试试孙武，就问他能否用兵法做些游戏。孙武郑重地回答说："用兵是一件很严肃的事情，直接关系人的利害存亡，是不能随便用来游戏或开玩笑的。"吴王很认同孙武的看法，但还是很想见识一下孙武的实际才能。吴王问道："先生能不能用吴宫的宫女来操演兵法？"孙武明白吴王的心意，就答应了吴王的请求。但他同时指出，妇人从未接触过战争，临阵多不严肃，恐怕吴王将来会后悔。吴王不以为意，认为只是演练一下，又没有什么危险，就满口答应了下来。

Duke Helyu wanted to see how well Sun Wu could command an army, and asked him to try in games. Sun Wu answered in seriousness, "Commanding an army is no laughing matter, for it means life and death. It is not for fun." Though the duke had the same opinion, he still wanted Sun Wu to demonstrate his talent. So the duke asked, "Sir, would you please try your methods on the maids in palace?" Sun Wu understood the duke's concern and would do so as the duke requested. But he warned the duke that these women knew nothing about war, and they would not behave as they were supposed to, and the duke might regret for what would happen. The duke assured himself that a drill was a drill, and nothing would happen.

◎ 兵场喧哗围观图
The excited spectators of the drill

故三军可夺气,将军可夺心。(《孙子兵法·军争篇》)

吴王和孙武约定次日上午到吴宫后边的演兵场操练女兵。第二天一早,孙武来到演兵场等候。演兵场周围已围满了看热闹的人,毕竟用宫女练兵,可是破天荒的头一回。

Duke Helyu and Sun Wu agreed to meet the next day morning to have the military drill. Sun Wu was at the drill ground well before its start. The ground was crowded with curious people: this is the first time ever that maids in palace would be seen in a military drill.

◎宫中佳丽列队图
Maids in the the drill

所谓古之善用兵者，能使敌人前后不相及，众寡不相恃，贵贱不相救，上下不相收，卒离而不集，兵合而不齐。（《孙子兵法·九地篇》）

吴王宫中选出的三百多名宫女陆续来到演兵场，莺声燕语，佳丽如云，引起围观众人浓厚的兴趣和热烈的讨论。孙武把宫女分成两队，每队一百八十人，按照高低顺序编制好队列，又让吴王的两名宠姬担任队长。

More than 300 maids picked for the drill came to the drill ground in succession. Their delicate figures and soft voice immediately became the focus of discussion. Sun Wu divided these young ladies into two groups, and 180 ladies in each group. The ladies stood in a line from the short to the tall. He made two of the duke's favorite concubines captains.

◎ 演前孙子立规图
Sunzi explaining the rules for drill

故善用兵者，譬如"率然"；"率然"者，常山之蛇也。击其首则尾至，击其尾则首至，击其中则首尾俱至。（《孙子兵法·九地篇》）

孙武站在指挥台上，开始仔细宣讲操练要领。他先伸出自己的左右手，然后指指自己的前心后背，让大家明白基本方向和行列知识。孙武说："每种动作都由鼓声统一指挥。鼓声指示向前，就要目视前方；鼓声指示向左，就看自己的左手；鼓声指示向右，就看自己的右手；鼓声指示向后，就转向自己后背方向。大家听明白了吗？"宫女们回答："听明白了。"

On the stand, Sun Wu explained in details the rules the maids must obey during the drill. He demonstrated the basic marching directions with his right and left hands, then the front and the back of his body. Sun Wu said, "Each move must be done in accordance with the beat of the drum. If the drum sound comes from the front, look forward; if it comes from the left, look to the left; if it comes from the right, look to the right. If it comes from the back, turn to the back. Got it?" "Yes," shouted the maids.

◎宫女嬉笑乱阵图
Playful carelessness in the drill

将军之事：静以幽，正以治。（《孙子兵法·九地篇》）

宣讲完毕，孙武命人拿来执法用的斧钺，竖立在演兵场的一侧，然后再次把军法演示一遍。宫女们已经不耐烦了。演练开始了。鼓声响起，指示士卒向右前进。宫女们从未经历过这种场面，既新奇又好笑，纷纷掩口而笑，完全不成队列。

After his explanation, Sun Wu ordered some axes to be erected on the sides of the ground, and then went over the rules again. The maids seemed already impatient. The drill started. The drum directed the procession to the right. Such a situation was so novel to the maids in the palace that they covered their mouth, laughing constantly. The formation was totally disrupted.

◎孙子训斥宠姬图
Sunzi criticizing the concubines

以治待乱,以静待哗,此治心者也。 (《孙子兵法·军争篇》)

吴王远远坐在观礼台上,心中暗自好笑。他想看看孙武如何应付这种局面。孙武命令鼓声停下来。他先严肃自责,然后再一次把军法详细申述一遍,又叫过两名队长,反复申斥,要求她们以身作则,听从号令。

Duke Helyu sat afar on the observation deck, smiling over the scene. He wanted to see how Sun Wu responded to such a situation. Sun Wu ordered the drum to stop. He criticized himself first and then explained the rules again. He summoned the two captains and asked them to be the role model.

◎孙子击鼓指挥图
Sunzi beating the drum to command

故其疾如风,其徐如林,侵掠如火,不动如山,难知如阴,动如雷震。
(《孙子兵法·军争篇》)

孙武这次亲自击鼓指挥,命令士卒向左方行进。官女们依然嬉笑如故。孙武大怒,两目圆睁,发上冲冠。

Sun Wu beat the drum himself to direct the drill formation to march left, but the maids laughed and talked as usual. Sun Wu was furious with this playful carelessness. He summoned the

他叫来执法官,问道:"按照军法,不服从军令该当何罪?"执法官回答:"其罪当斩!"

chief, and asked, "How do we punish those who do not obey the rules?" "Behead!" answered the chief.

◎孙子拒情斩姬图
**The captains beheaded**

涂有所不由，军有所不击，城有所不攻，地有所不争，君命有所不受。
(《孙子兵法·九变篇》)

孙武面色铁青，毫不犹豫地命人将两名队长推下去斩首。吴王大惊，忙派人传令孙武，请求手下留情。他说："寡人知道将军能用兵了。没有这两位美姬，寡人食不甘味，请将军看在寡人的面上放了两人。"孙武义正词严地回答："庙堂之上，大王命我带队演兵，虽是女兵，却君无戏言。孙武今天将兵在外，君命有所不受。"说完，就下令当场斩了两名女队长。

Sun Wu's face settled on an ugly greenish white. He wanted to have the two captains beheaded. The duke was so shocked that he sent messengers to plead with Sun Wu. The duke said, "I now know you are capable of commanding a troop. But I cannot eat well and sleep well without these two belles. Please pardon them for my sake." Sun Wu refused flatly, "When Your Majesty asked me to have a military drill, you made it no laughing matter. A duke must mean what he means even though the soldiers are maids. I'm the general-in-command today, with all the due respect to Your Majesty, I call the shots today." Saying that, he had the two captains beheaded.

◎宫女整齐练兵图
A real drill

视卒如婴儿，故可与之赴深溪；视卒如爱子，故可与之俱死。厚而不能使，爱而不能令，乱而不能治，譬若骄子，不可用也。（《孙子兵法·地形篇》）

孙武又挑了两名宫女做队长，亲自擂鼓，继续操练。这一次，众女兵动作出乎意料地整齐划一，进退回旋、跪起爬滚，无不中规中矩，再也没有一丝懈怠。孙武向吴王通报操练情况："女兵队伍已经训练好，无论大王让她们做任何事情，她们都会按您的命令去做，绝不会有任何含糊。"

Sun Wu then picked another two maids to be the captains. He beat the drum himself and continued the drill. This time these women acted as one person upon whatever the orders they were given, marching forward or withdrawing back, kneeling or crawling. They performed every task as required and showed no sluggishness at all. Sun Wu reported to the duke, "The soldiers are ready, and they will do whatever Your Majesty ask them to do without any delay."

◎孙子辞别吴王图
Sunzi bidding farewell to Duke Helyu

主孰有道？将孰有能？天地孰得？法令孰行？兵众孰强？士卒孰练？赏罚孰明？吾以此知胜负矣。(《孙子兵法·计篇》)

吴王怒气未息，冷冷地对孙武说："请将军回去休息，寡人心绪不佳，不愿再看下去了。"孙武淡然一笑："原来大王只是喜欢书上的空道理，并不想真正实行它。"然后他告辞回到自己的馆舍，准备离开。伍子胥劝阻了他。

Duke Helyu was still in the spasm of anger, and said to Sun Wu coldly, "You may as well go for a rest, General. I'm not in a good mood to watch the drill." Sun Wu smiled calmly, "Your Majesty prefers to study the theories rather than practise them." He then went back to his place and packed up. Wu Zixu persuaded him not to.

◎吴王纳谏释嫌图
Duke Helyu and Sun Wu settling differences

计利以听，乃为之势，以佐其外。势者，因利而制权也。(《孙子兵法·计篇》)

吴王失去两名爱姬，当面不好发作，回去后一连几天都烦躁不安。伍子胥进谏："兵者凶事，不能空试。诛伐如果不行，兵道就会不明。大王如欲兴兵伐楚，威震天下，除了孙将军还能有谁呢？"吴王终于解开心结，决定亲自前去挽留孙武。孙武向吴王谢罪，并解释杀吴王美姬的理由："令行禁止，赏罚分明，是为将治军的通则，也是克敌制胜的基础。"一番深谈，吴王怒气全消，尽释前嫌。

Duke Helyu lost two of his favorite concubines. He suppressed his frustration so hard that he felt restless for days. Wu Zixu said, "War means life and death. One is not supposed to make fun of it. If there is no punishment, orders will not be obeyed. If Your Majesty wants to attack the State of Chu and obtain the hegemonic position, who else can help you except General Sun?" The duke finally let go his grudge against Sun Wu, and decided himself to ask Sun to stay. Sun Wu apologized for his offense and explained, "Every order should be executed without fail, and offenders receive their punishments which they rightly deserved. And this should be the way to command an army and defeat the enemies." The duke was soothed and he agreed to forgive and forget.

◎孙武练兵强国图
Sun Wu training the troops

投之亡地然后存,陷之死地然后生。夫众陷于害,然后能为胜败。
(《孙子兵法·九地篇》)

吴王决定正式拜孙武为将军。在孙武的严格训练下,吴国军队很快成为一支纪律严明、骁勇善战的无敌之师,为日后吴国争霸之路奠定了坚实的基础。

Duke Helyu officially appointed Sun Wu as general. Under Sun Wu's strict training, the army of Wu became a well-disciplined and fiercest army, making the State of Wu a rising power possible.

◎吴国兴兵伐楚图
The State of Wu attacking the State of Chu

故善用兵者，屈人之兵而非战也，拔人之城而非攻也，毁人之国而非久也，必以全争于天下，故兵不顿而利可全，此谋攻之法也。（《孙子兵法·谋攻篇》）

阖闾三年（前512），吴国兴兵伐楚。吴王命伍子胥、孙武为将，夺取舒城，斩杀了前吴王僚逃亡到楚国的两个胞弟。吴王想乘机进攻楚国都城郢。孙武认为时机并不成熟，就劝谏吴王说："不可，士卒们太过疲惫，大王还是再等等吧。"

In the third year under Duke Helyu's reign (512 B. C.), the State of Wu launched an attack on the State of Chu. Duke Helyu appointed Wu Zixu and Sun Wu as generals. They conquered Shucheng and killed two brothers of Duke Liao, the former duke of Wu. Duke Helyu wanted to seize the opportunity to conquer the capital city of Chu, but Sun Wu thought the time was not ripe yet, and advised the duke by saying, "Not now. The soldiers are too tired. We might wait for another time in the future."

◎孙子疲楚观变图
Sunzi waiting for the timing

故用兵之法，十则围之，五则攻之，倍则分之，敌则能战之，少则能逃之，不若则能避之。故小敌之坚，大敌之擒也。(《孙子兵法·谋攻篇》)

楚国是传统的强国，楚昭王是一位仁厚君主，令尹子常刚刚又诛杀了奸臣费无忌，大快人心。此时的楚国吏治清明，万众一心。吴王自己也知道现在时机并不成熟，就听从了孙武的建议，收兵回国。在此期间，孙武一方面精心操练兵马，一方面帮吴王定下了灭楚的战略方针：一是疲楚误楚，二是静观其变。

The State of Chu was in tradition a great power. Duke Zhao of Chu was kind and benevolent, and their minister Zichang just killed the treacherous minister Fei Wuji. People in Chu were happy to live in a harmonious state and they were united in one heart. Duke Helyu knew it was not the right time to attack Chu, and thus followed Sun Wu's advice and withdrew the troops. Sun Wu wasted no time to train the troops intensively, and at the same time he laid out the strategy for the duke: tire out Chu and mislead Chu; wait to find its weakness.

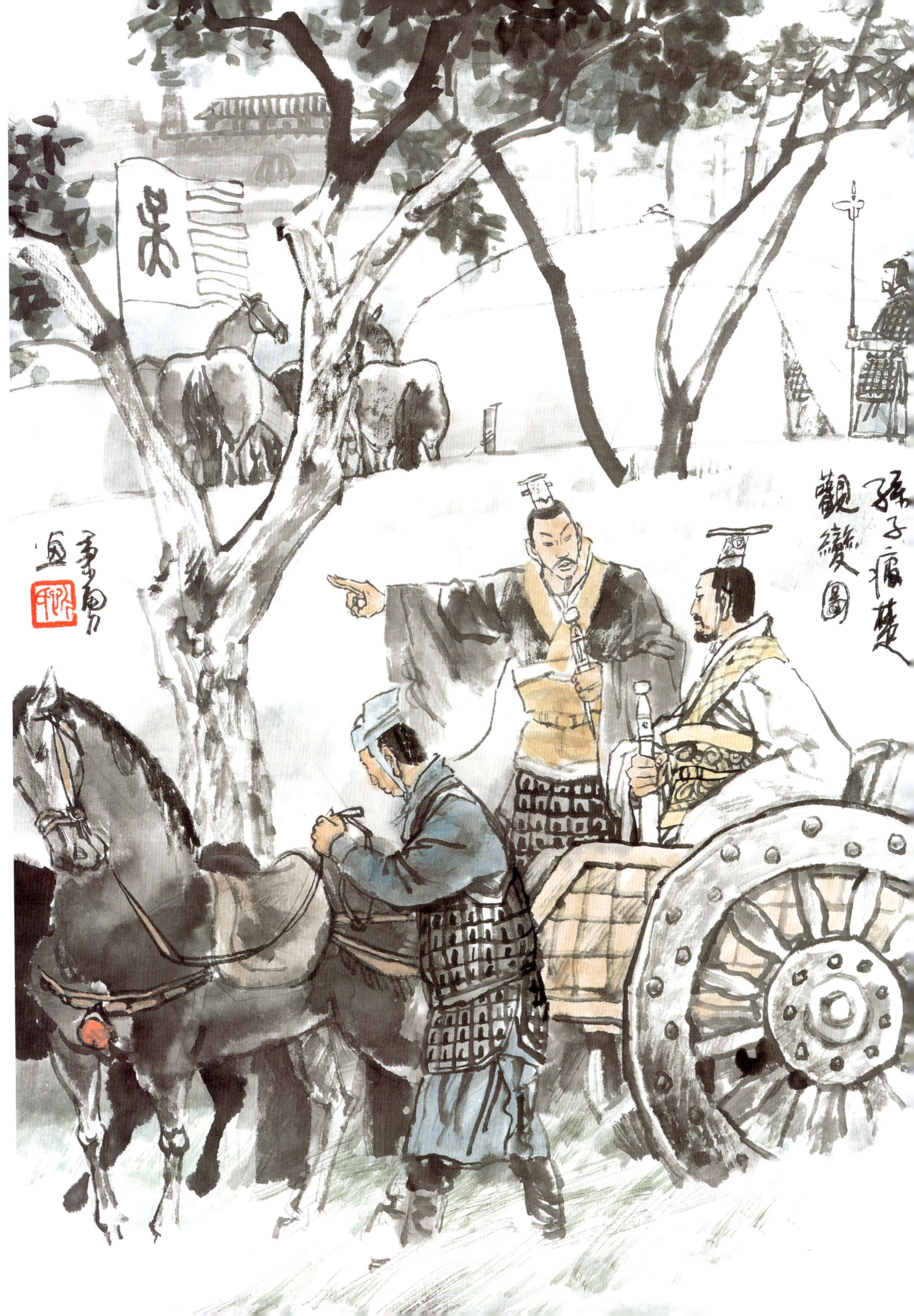
觀變圖

◎ 子常索贿蒙君图
Zichang asking for bribes

夫未战而庙算胜者，得算多也；未战而庙算不胜者，得算少也。多算胜，少算不胜，而况无算乎！吾以此观之，胜负见矣。（《孙子兵法·计篇》）

阖闾六年（前509），蔡国国君蔡昭侯朝觐楚王，命人制作了两枚玉佩和两件狐裘大衣，十分精美，其中一佩一裘献给楚王，自己留用另一份。楚国令尹子常为人十分贪婪，派人向蔡昭侯索取另一份。蔡昭侯不给，子常便找借口非法扣留他达三年之久。同年，唐国国君唐成公朝觐楚王，驾车的两匹宝马神骏非常，子常垂涎三尺，必欲得之而后快。唐成公不给，子常如法炮制，同样将他扣留了三年。

In the sixth year under Duke Helyu's reign (509 B. C.), Duke Zhao of Cai visited the State of Chu. He had two jade ornaments and two fur coats made for this visit, one ornament and one coat presented for the duke of Chu, and the other kept for himself. Zichang, the minister of Chu, was so greedy that he demanded to have what were meant for the duke of Cai. Duke Zhao of Cai refused, and Zichang detained him for three years. In the same year, Duke Cheng of Tang visited Chu, and the carriage he rode had two handsome horses. Zichang wanted to have the horses, but Duke Cheng refused. Zichang also detained him for three years.

◎蔡、唐贡宝救主图
Tributes paid for a journey home

故知胜有五：知可以战与不可以战者胜，识众寡之用者胜，上下同欲者胜，以虞待不虞者胜，将能而君不御者胜。此五者，知胜之道也。（《孙子兵法·谋攻篇》）

阖闾八年（前507）冬天，蔡、唐两国大臣设法说服本国国君，把玉佩、狐裘和宝马献给子常，蔡昭侯、唐成公才得以归国。两国对楚国的不满情绪达到了极点。

In the winter of the eighth year under Duke Helyu's reign (507 B. C.), the ministers of Tang and Cai tried to persuade their dukes to let Zichang have what he desired, and then their dukes eventually came back home. The resentment against Chu had never been so strong in Tang and Cai.

◎孙子献策奇袭图
Sunzi`s proposal

故上兵伐谋，其次伐交，其次伐兵，其下攻城。（《孙子兵法·谋攻篇》）

阖闾九年（前506），吴王认为吴国实力已经足够强大，便旧话重提，与伍子胥、孙武二人商讨伐楚大计。孙武展开地图，为吴王分析两国形势："楚国地大兵强，郢都又相距遥远，从楚国境内正面进攻郢都太过凶险，必须从外围绕道奇袭才有成功的希望。而要绕道，唐、蔡两国是必经之地，因而必须得到两国的支持才行。"

In the ninth year under Duke Helyu's reign (506 B. C), the duke of Wu thought his country was powerful enough, and he brought up again the issue of attacking Chu for discussion with Wu Zixu and Sun Wu. Sun Wu unfolded the map and analyzed the situations of the two countries: "Chu is a strong state with vast land, and its capital is far from the border. It is too risky if we launch a frontal attack to capture its capital. We have to take a detour to launch a surprise attack on Chu, but Tang and Cai are the two countries we have to cut through. We need to have their support."

◎吴楚夹岸对峙图
The troops of Wu confronting the troops of Chu

兵之情主速，乘人之不及，由不虞之道，攻其所不戒也。（《孙子兵法·九地篇》）

孙武苦苦等待的机会终于来了。这年秋天，怀恨在心的蔡国灭了楚国的附庸国沈国。楚国兴兵围蔡，誓报沈国之仇。蔡国向吴国求救。经过孙武等人的详细谋划后，吴王阖闾御驾亲征，以伍子胥、孙武为将军，以胞弟夫概为先锋，率三万水陆大军，以救蔡为名，秘密向蔡国进发。吴军遵循孙武"出其不意，攻其不备"的指导思想，秘密抵达淮汭，与唐、蔡两国会师，然后迅速通过楚国北部大隧、直辕、冥阨三道险关，挺进汉水东岸，与楚军夹岸对峙。

The opportunity Sun Wu had been waiting for finally came. This autumn, the State of Cai conquered Chu's vassal state, Shen. Chu surrounded Cai in revenge for Shen. Cai asked Wu for help. After Sun Wu's careful planning, Duke Helyu led the troops with Wu Zixu and Sun Wu as generals and his own younger brother Fugai as the vanguard. The 30,000-solider troops set out from both river and land in the name of rescuing Cai. To take Chu by surprise, they arrived in Huairui secretly. They joined the troops of Tang and Cai, and broke through three strategic passes in the north of Chu. Finally, Wu's troops made their way to Han River, confronting Chu on the other side of the bank.

◎ 诱敌深入决战图
**Luring the enemy in deep**

夫地形者，兵之助也。料敌制胜，计险厄远近，上将之道也。（《孙子兵法·地形篇》）

楚国令尹子常并没有把吴军放在眼里，要求渡过汉水与吴国军队作战。孙武利用子常轻敌的心理，采取将计就计、后退诱敌、伺机决战的对策，一举击败楚军。随后，在孙武的指挥下，吴军在小别山与大别山之间与楚军周旋，屡次挫败楚国的精锐部队，极大地打击了楚军的士气。

Chu's minister Zichang did not take Wu's attack seriously. He wanted the troops to cross the river to attack Wu's troops squarely. Sun Wu took advantage of Zichang's negligence and eagerness, withdrew his troops to lure Chu in deep, and finally defeated Chu. Then, under Sun Wu's leadership, Wu's troops waged battles in mountains against Chu's troops. Their repeated victories greatly undermined Chu's morale.

◎孙、伍备战柏举图
Sunzi and Wu Zixu planning for the coming battle in Boju

故战道必胜，主曰无战，必战可也；战道不胜，主曰必战，无战可也。故进不求名，退不避罪，唯人是保，而利合于主，国之宝也。（《孙子兵法·地形篇》）

十一月，子常带领屡战屡败的楚军退缩到郢都的门户、军事重地柏举，再也没有后退的余地，决心背水一战。吴国军队胜利在望，群情振奋。孙武告诫吴王不可掉以轻心，并与伍子胥一起，为柏举之役制订了详细的作战计划。

In lunar November, Zichang and his troops retreated to a place called Boju, an important gateway to the capital city, where Zichang was forced back against the wall. The troops of Wu were so excited to see the victory coming, but Sun Wu warned Duke Helyu not to take it lightly. Sun Wu worked out a plan with Wu Zixu for the coming battle in Boju.

◎ 夫概孤勇出战图
Fugai leading the fight

凡战者，以正合，以奇胜。故善出奇者，无穷如天地，不竭如江海。
（《孙子兵法·势篇》）

第二天清晨，吴王阖闾的胞弟夫概请令出战。他认为楚国令尹子常刻薄寡恩、贪得无厌，手下将士不肯替他卖命，此次出战一定能大败楚军。桀骜不驯的夫概，不顾哥哥的阻拦，带领自己的五千士兵径自出战。夫概此举打乱了事前的作战计划，所幸楚军此前屡败，早已成惊弓之鸟，受此突袭，便被一举击溃。

In the next morning, Duke Helyu's younger brother Fugai asked to be the first to fight. He thought that Zichang was so mean and avaricious that no soldier would be willing to die for Zichang, and he must be able to defeat Zichang. The arrogant and unruly Fugai totally ignored his brother's protest, and led 5,000 soldiers of his own to fight. Though Fugai's move disrupted the previously agreed deployment, the repeatedly defeated Chu could not stand up against this sudden attack, and totally collapsed.

◎乘胜追击溃楚图
Defeating Chu with victorious pursuit

*故善动敌者，形之，敌必从之；予之，敌必取之。以利动之，以卒待之。（《孙子兵法·势篇》）*

孙武当机立断，指挥吴军乘胜追击，先后在清发水、雍澨等地追上楚军，给楚军残部以多次沉重打击。楚军主帅子常潜逃郑国，吴军取得柏举之战的重大胜利。失去柏举的屏障，郢都完全暴露在吴军的铁骑之下。楚昭王一面组织兵力拦截吴军，一面仓皇撤离郢都。孙武率领吴军长驱直入，势如破竹，五战五捷，终于在十一月底前攻下郢都。这一仗，在孙武的精心组织和策划下，吴军千里奇袭，以三万兵力破楚二十万兵力，创造了中国战争史上的奇迹。

Sun Wu ordered his troops to continue their victorious pursuit without delay. They caught up with Chu's troops and defeated their remaining forces. As Zichang fled to the State of Zheng, Wu won the battle in Boju. When Boju was taken, the capital of Chu was vulnerable to the attack from Wu. While organizing more soldiers to defend, Duke Zhao of Chu fled from the capital in panic. Sun Wu and his troops swept town after town, penetrating Chu with sweeping force. After five successive victories, they conquered the capital of Chu in lunar November. Under Sun Wu's careful planning, the 30,000 Wu army defeated 200,000 Chu army, thus making a miracle in Chinese military history.

◎包胥秦庭哭救图
Baoxu crying for help

故备前则后寡，备后则前寡，备左则右寡，备右则左寡，无所不备，则无所不寡。寡者备人者也，众者使人备己者也。（《孙子兵法·虚实篇》）

楚国大夫申包胥千里迢迢赶到秦国求救，秦人不许。申包胥站在秦国宫门外不吃不喝，一连哭了七天七夜，终于感动了秦哀公。秦国答应发兵车五百乘抗吴救楚。

Shen Baoxu, a minister of Chu, went all the way to the State of Qin to ask for help. Qin turned a deaf ear to his plea. Shen Baoxu wailed at the outside of Qin's court for seven days and nights without eating and drinking. Duke Ai of Qin was so moved and promised to send 500 carriages, including 50,000 people, for their rescue.

◎吴王回师平叛图
**A coup at home**

故经之以五,校之以计,而索其情:一曰道,二曰天,三曰地,四曰将,五曰法。
(《孙子兵法·计篇》)

吴王阖闾被巨大的胜利冲昏了头脑,不听孙武尽快班师回国的建议,一心想要抓住楚昭王。夫概趁这个空档,偷偷回到吴国自立为王。内外交困的吴王最终还是听从孙武的劝告,挥师归国平叛。夫概不是孙武等人的敌手,仓皇败走,逃到楚国避难。

Duke Helyu was so overwhelmed by the victory that he wanted nothing else but to catch Duke Zhao of Chu. He did not want to return home as Sun Wu advised. Taking advantage of Helyu's absence from the royal court, Fugai, the duke's younger brother, went back to Wu and crowned himself duke. Beset with troubles internally and externally, Duke Helyu had to follow Sun Wu's advice. He returned to Wu to crack down the coup. Being no rival to Sun Wu, Fugai escaped to Chu.

◎孙子功名受托图
Entrusting the care of Fuchai

知彼知己，百战不殆；不知彼而知己，一胜一负；不知彼，不知己，每战必殆
（《孙子兵法·谋攻篇》）

两年后，吴王阖闾再次任命孙武、伍子胥为将，辅佐太子夫差兴兵伐楚，攻取楚国的番地。孙武名动天下，楚国被吓破了胆，将都城迁到了鄀。又过了三年，吴王阖闾在与越国的一次战斗中受伤，不治而亡。临终前，他嘱咐孙武等人辅佐太子夫差，完成自己未竟的事业。

Two years later, Duke Helyu appointed Sun Wu and Wu Zixu as generals again to help his son Fuchai to attack Chu's vassal state. Sun Wu's reputation frightened Chu off. Chu relocated their capital in Ruo. Another three years passed, Duke Helyu died from a wound in a battle against the State of Yue. On his deathbed, he entrusted his son Fuchai to Sun Wu, and asked him and other officials to help Fuchai complete his unfinished mission.

◎孙、伍辅吴称霸图
Wu being the dominant power with the two assistants

凡用兵之法，全国为上，破国次之；全军为上，破军次之；全旅为上，破旅次之；全卒为上，破卒次之；全伍为上，破伍次之。（《孙子兵法·谋攻篇》）

孙武与伍子胥一起，辅佐新一代吴王夫差，向南打败越国，为夫差报了杀父之仇；向北威震齐、晋，最终成就了吴国的霸主地位。

Sun Wu, together with Wu Zixu, assisted Fuchai, the new duke of Wu, fought all the way to the south to defeat the State of Yue, and avenged his father's death. In the north, Wu's power was terrified the State of Qi and the State of Jin. Wu eventually obtained the hegemonic position.

◎兵圣兵书流芳图
*The Art of War*

是故百战百胜，非善之善者也；不战而屈人之兵，善之善者也。
(《孙子兵法·谋攻篇》)

孙武的一生，除了赫赫战功以外，更重要的是他给后人留下了一部前无古人的军事奇书《孙子兵法》。《孙子兵法》全书有13篇6000余字，是我国现存最早的兵书，在中国乃至世界军事领域产生了深远的影响。

Apart from his victories in the battlefield, Sun Wu left behind him an unprecedented book *The Art of War* about military strategies. *The Art of War*, including 13 articles ,6000 words, is the earliest extant book on the military strategy in China, exerting far-reaching impact on the military area at home and abroad.

◎王者之道普世图
Words of wisdom

夫兵形像水，水之形避高而趋下，兵之形避实而击虚，水因地而制流，兵因敌而制胜。故兵无常势，水无常形，能因敌变化而取胜者，谓之神。
（《孙子兵法·虚实篇》）

《孙子兵法》留给世人的绝不仅仅是关于战争的各种阴谋阳谋，更多的是如何对待战争的智慧。正如孙武所说，战争固然需要诡诈的手段，但慎重对待战争，不骄不躁、知己知彼、不战而屈人之兵才是王者之道。孙武的哲学精神早已融入我们中华民族爱好和平、不畏强权的民族性格当中。

What *The Art of War* leaves us is more wisdom than tactics and tricks about the war. To quote Sun Wu, it is unavoidable to play some tricks and employ some tactics in the war, but war is something we should try to avoid. No arrogance, no rashness, knowing both your part and your enemy, and defeating the enemy without engaging a war. These should be the military leadership. Sun Wu's philosophy has long been embedded in our peace-loving and power-defying Chinese character.

## 作者手记

追溯中华文明的源头，我们总能发现诸子百家的足迹；谈论东方艺术的精粹，离不开中国传统绘画。两者互为载体，比翼齐飞。将灿烂的中华文明通过国画连环画展现在世人面前，无疑是一件非常有意义的事情。在诸子百家中，孙子是个极有特点的人物。一部被誉为"百世兵家之师、东方兵学鼻祖"的《孙子兵法》，凝聚着孙子的智慧、思想和文化，是中华文明的重要智慧根基和源泉。

历经艰辛的创作，终于完成了这套画稿，交稿的一刻，竟有种如释重负的感觉。虽然我曾经创作过《东周列国》等古典连环画，但要站在以国风国韵展现中华文化的高度去塑造孙子，责任之大，非全身心投入不可。于是，我花了较多的时间查阅资料，重新了解孙子的生平，认真研读《孙子兵法》，努力从字里行间获得启示，寻找和捕捉孙子的视觉形象，并根据画面的需要调整原始文稿。在艺术处理上，我运用自己熟悉的国画、连环画的笔墨与线条，半工半写，既有大笔的挥洒，又不乏细节的雕琢，相对于传统章法，在构图上略带装饰性，融入了更多的现代元素。

我想，每个时代对于孙子这个历史人物都会有不同的理解，留有不同的视觉印象，历史人物是活在当代人的脑海中的。如是，则还原是为了解读，创作更是一种塑造，我们无须回避时代的印痕，也不必拘泥于孙子的原始形象和传统的艺术形式。我试图以这种具有独特个性并带有时代印记的艺术形式与读者共鸣，不知能被接受否？

乙未年立冬

# The Artist's Words

When we trace back the origin of Chinese civilization, we can always track the footprints of the great thinkers; when we talk about the essence of Oriental art, we cannot fail to mention traditional Chinese painting. They are inseparable company to each other. It is very meaningful to present the world the brilliant Chinese civilization through traditional Chinese painting. Among the great thinkers, Sunzi is a very special one. *The Art of War*, a military masterpiece "founding the military science in the East, showing examples for all armies" , is a brainchild of Sunzi. *The Art of War* epitomizes his wisdom and thinking, and is one of the cornerstones of Chinese culture.

I felt so relieved when I completed this task after much creative agony. Though I created historical picture books such as *The Stories of States in Eastern Zhou Dynasty*, to delineate Sunzi from the perspective of Chinese culture is physically and intellectually demanding. I spent quite some time collecting materials, sorting through Sunzi's life, and reading in a very careful manner *The Art of War*. I read between the lines to capture inspiration for a seeable Sunzi, and I revised the captions to fit in with my painting. In terms of painting skills, I employed with ease pen and ink, line and brush in my fine brushwork and freehand brushwork. Both broad brushwork and careful attention to the details contribute to the portraying of Sunzi. Moreover, unlike traditional practice, I included more modern ornamental elements in the composition of my painting.

In my understanding, each era allows a different interpretation about a historical figure, and each era allows a different visual construction of Sunzi. If my understanding is correct, reproduction is interpretation, and creation is recreation. We don't have to avoid the impression of this era, and we don't have to limit ourselves to the stereotypes of Sunzi and the traditional art form. I try to relate to my audience in an art form with characteristics of the era we live in as well as my personal touch. Could I have the response I expect?

Xin Bingyong<br>Winter, 2015

# 后记

中国国家主席习近平在谈及中华文化时，深刻地指出："中华优秀传统文化已经成为中华民族的基因，植根在中国人内心，潜移默化影响着中国人的思想方式和行为方式。"厚重、灿烂的中华传统文化，如何借由一种生动、直观、亲切的方式走进读者，尤其是海外读者的阅读视野中，一直是文化界关注、思索的问题。当《诸子百家国风画传》丛书带着"传承、创新、中国风"的鲜明印迹从上海出发，正是希望由此探索向世界传播、普及中国优秀传统文化的新方式和新渠道。

上海，作为国际文化大都市，通过源源不断地推出文化交流精品，成为海外读者了解中国、感受中国的一扇精彩窗口。发源于上海的连环画艺术，则以其浓郁、独特的中国韵味深受国内外读者的欢迎。两年前，以传承、振兴中国连环画艺术为主旨的上海海派连环画中心甫一成立，即在上海市政府新闻办的指导、创意下，联合发起策划一套以国风连环画为载体、契合"读图时代"特点的《诸子百家国风画传》丛书，并得到了国务院新闻办公室、中共上海市委宣传部的大力支持，以及山东、河南省政府新闻办和相关诸子故里的密切协作。

尤为可贵的是，国内著名国画家郭德福、李维定、赵明钧、邵家声、忻秉勇为淋漓再现智者先贤而实地采风，遍览典籍，泼墨挥毫，探寻中国文化符号世界化表达的崭新方式。画家们数易其稿，精益求精，创作出让人耳目一新、形神兼备的诸子形象。画传不仅选取诸子生平中最具典型意义的事件，还注意表现鲜有人关注的诸子日常生活。画传想让读者感知的不只是存在于文献、传说里的古之圣贤，更是身边熟悉亲切、可以答疑解惑的智者。

我们衷心希望，这套充满哲理智慧与中国艺术美质的丛书能够成为连接当代与中华传统的文化桥梁。希望中华文化的寻源之旅能让每一个中国人寻回精神归属，也让海外读者从另一蹊径了解中国文化之美。

《诸子百家国风画传》丛书编委会

二〇一四年九月